BOBCATS

Ghostly Elusive

Dr. Richard A. NeSmith

Love of Nature Series

ISSUE 4

Applied Principles of Education & Learning

APE-Learning

http://richardnesmith.obior.cc

© 2020 Richard A. NeSmith
Love of Nature Series

dr.nesmith@gmail.com

April 2021

Dr. Richard A. NeSmith

ISBN: 9798666290385

FLESCH-KINCAID GRADE LEVEL: 8.3

Bobcats
(*Lynx rufus*)

Mysterious, mystical, and elusive, and solitary. Revered and respected by American Natives. They were believed to be able to impose wisdom but only visible when wanted to be seen. As they are generally known, the American bobcats are from the family Felidae and the genus Lynx. They are also known as *red lynx*. So a lynx and bobcat are cousins and very similar in appearance but are not the same species. The lynx is of the genus/

species, *Lynx lynx*, whereas the bobcat is *Lynx rufus*. Differences, however, are difficult, even for the best of naturalists. They often have brown, brownish to yellow-orange variegated (multi-colored) coats, but some are reddish. They have a white underbelly and, of course, the short, black-tipped tail.

The tail is vital to recognizing a bobcat from a lynx. The tip of the lynx's tail is entirely black like as though it has been dipped into a bucket of black ink. In contrast, a bobcat's tail is black on top and completely white on the underneath side. These *felines* are medium-sized cats with long, tufted ears (shorter on bobcats than on lynxes) and a short, bobbed tail. The short tail is a natural result of their genetic makeup. The tufts (a bunch or collection of hairs) on the ears seem to help identify bobcats and lynxes, which we will consider later. There are 13 recognized subspecies, with the bobcats being the smallest and the largest being the

Eurasian lynx.

Range

Bobcats are native (endemic) to North America from southern Canada, most of the contiguous United States to Oaxaca in Mexico. They are widely distributed and abundant, with an estimated population of between 2.3 to 3.5 million. They have been increasing in North America since the 1990s. They are currently the most abundant wildcat in the United States. Even with such a large number in nature, they are seldom seen, thus the nickname, *ghost of the woods*. They establish a home range, and though never overlapping with other females, the females' territory may overlap those of the males'. Contrary, male bobcats' territories do often overlap ranges. A male's territories can range up to 30 square miles, whereas the female's home range is approximately 5 square miles. Bobcats mark their boundaries with several methods, including claw marks and deposits of urine or feces.

These creatures tend to be solitary, shy, and avoid people. Some have even referred to them as ***ghostly elusive*** mammals. Part of this reason is that they are ***nocturnal*** (hunting at night) and generally sleeping during the day. Other reasons for their obscurity have to do with their keen sense of sight, hearing, and smell, all helping them catch prey and avoid predators and humans. They do a lot of roaming. Though seldom seen and rarely aggressive, bobcats with rabies can be erratic in their behavior and can attack humans. In some regions, bobcats are hunted or trapped extensively for sport and fur. Still, some populations have proven resilient though declining in some areas.

They are very adaptable predators, usually living in wooded areas. However, some are found in semi-desert regions, urban and forest edges, mountains, and wetlands/

swampland environments.

Characteristics

Bobcats have unique black bars on their forelegs and black-tipped stubby bobbed tails. Bobcats are about twice the size of an ordinary house cat (approximately 11-30 pounds). They range in size from about 26 to 41 inches from head to tail. The tail may only be from 4 to 12 inches long. In the wild, they live from 10-12 years of age. The oldest wild bobcat on record was 16 years old, and the oldest captive bobcat lived to be 32 years of age.

The bobcat's coat color and patterns are unique and vary by individual. Some have well-defined rosette spots on their bodies, some are freckled, and some have no spots at all. Bobcat's coat pattern is like fingerprints and does not change from birth onward. Coat patterns are unique and can be used to identify individuals. The coat color blends so well in most flora (plant life) that it is impossible to see them.

The eyes of a bobcat look very different than those typical eyes of cats. Their eyes do *not* have vertical slit pupils like domestic cats. Bobcats often have a crisp, white lining around their eyes, but not all cats share this coloration. Bobcats have *round pupils*, hazel or gold in color, though many of the kittens have blue-colored eyes.

Around the face and neck region is a frill area of hair called the *ruff*. From which we get our word for *ruffles*, which is used to describe a frilly collar. This tuff of hair seems to be connected in such a way as to be controlled by the bobcat and often reflects upon their mood or disposition, like that of the back (nape) of a dog's neck. In bobcats, this ruff can make their cheeks appear puffy, or they can appear more slicked or smoothed back.

Once bobcats have reached eight weeks of age, all have

black ears with a distinctive white patch in the center. Some adults may have a small tuft on the tips of their ears, though this may not always be obvious. Bobcat tufts are shorter than those of the lynx.

The bobcats' hind legs are comparably longer than their front legs and are especially noticeable compared to house cats. The benefit of the longer back legs is the amount of power and spring provided by the muscles and the backbone's extra curvature. Their full padded paws allow them to walk *silently*, even among dead, dried leaves. Therefore, faster running, jumping, and extraordinary leaping characteristics are used in stealth hunting and avoiding being hunted.

Also, unlike housecats, bobcats do not make the same noises or sounds. Instead, they make a series of grunts, snarls, whines, growls and communicate these as if a language of their own. Some sounds seem to be given in sequence, and a whine or a grunt can start at one pitch and end on another. When they do growl, they sound much larger and more ferocious than expected.

Diet

Bobcats are top *visual* opportunistic predators in many

ecosystems. They have a significant effect on the biome in which they live. As **carnivores**, they hunt by stealth. That is, they sneak up silently upon their prey, then deliver a deathblow by leaping and pouncing on them. That leap can cover a 10-12 foot distance. Though bobcats do not do a lot of running, they can reach speeds of 25 to 30 mph in short bursts. The main hunting tactic is its ability to lie in wait for prey.

They exhibit an aggressive hunting style and can take enormous leaps to catch their prey. Bobcats can kill prey much larger than themselves but usually eat rabbits, birds, mice, squirrels, and other smaller game. Though preferring

rabbits and hares, it also hunts insects, chickens, reptiles, geese, and other birds (like turkey), small rodents, and *especially* young deer. Prey selection generally depends on location and habitat, season, and abundance. Bobcats have been known to prey on small pets, such as dogs and cats.

Habitat

A habitat is an environment in which an animal lives. Bobcats have adapted well and tend to be successful in most domains. They make a home in dens abandoned by others, and often bobcats have more than one den. Though thriving, some bobcats have become vulnerable to local extinction (called **extirpation**) by regular predators, including foxes, coyotes, mountain lions, wolves, large owls, eagles, and hawks. Bobcat kittens are especially vulnerable. Many bobcats fall prey to disease, parasites, predators, and automobiles. Approximately 20% of young bobcats are lost each year. Humans and their domesticated dogs are the only real threat to bobcats.

Behavior

Female bobcats are solitary and seldom associate with the opposite sex except during breeding season. They rarely make noise and are rarely heard. They are territorial and night-creatures, hunting at night, and continuously marking their territory as they make rounds. It is not uncommon for a bobcat to travel seven miles every night. They are excellent climbers and are often active at dusk

(***crepuscular***), meaning they are most active during twilight (dawn and dusk), and throughout the night.

Bobcats, along with other species, help to keep the ecosystem balanced. Ecosystems that become short on predators cause an environment to have fewer consumers in the food chain. This imbalance would cause a rapid increase in the population size of the typical prey. An overpopulation in such a situation would then cause the over-taxing of food resources. This *domino effect* would lead to more unsatisfactory conditions for other animals, resulting in starvation or death.

Ecosystems out of synch, as such, will eventually lead to low birth rates and high mortality and will cause populations to crash. Ultimately, even the plant life is affected. So, bobcats play an essential role in nutrient cycling and in helping maintain a healthy ecosystem. Some

have suggested bobcats might well be *keystone* species. Ecosystems that become stressed due to *urban sprawl* and the constant development of housing, industry, and businesses, face unhealthy ecological circumstances that eventually create a dying biome. More needs to be done to plan and protect large natural tracks of land to ensure this does not happen.

Reproduction

Bobcats usually begin breeding by age two. Females, however, may start as early as their first year. Once establishing a home range, females then become receptive to breeding. A dominant male, usually larger, will travel with a female, mating several times, generally from winter to early spring. Gestation lasts for 60 days. Bobcats have multiple mates, meaning they do not stay with a particular partner. When bobcats pair, they have various mating rituals, including bumping, chasing, and ambushing one another. Often the typically silent bobcat may, during courtship, let out screams, hisses, or sounds. Mature

bobcats can bear offspring their entire lives.

Females raise the young by themselves without the male's assistance. Usually, the litter has from one to four kittens born in April or May, nearly 60-70 days after pregnancy (gestation). The female bobcat (called a *queen*) becomes independent of the male bobcat (named a *tom*). She will give birth in some confined location such as a den, cave, or even a hollow log. By the 9th or 10th day, the kittens open their eyes. By week 4, the kittens are active and exploring their surroundings. By the end of the second month, they are weaned. Three to five months following, they begin to travel with the mother,

learning how to hunt for themselves by the end of the fall of their first year. The juvenile cats leave their mother around 8 to 11 months before the mother gives birth to another litter. Shortly following this, most young bobcats will depart and disperse to establish their own territory.

Miscellaneous

Of all the wild cats in North America, the bobcat has the most extensive range and is also the most abundant. However, as fur became more expensive in the past, bobcat populations decreased in the wild from human hunting and trapping. This drop became very significant in the 1970s. So for the last 50 years, laws were put into place, helping protect such population fluctuations. In most states, the pelts of bobcat skins must be registered or tagged by proper game-life authorities. Bobcats are thriving well in North America and Mexico, especially in dense vegetation areas with plenty of prey.

The legends and mysteries of bobcats and their secret lives live on today. But bobcats have become some of the most adaptive and successful animals in North American forests. Given the denser forest and ample prey, that has grown to be the largest cat population of all, and yet, they are seldom seen and rarely heard. If you see one, you will never forget it. And, you will know you were given a special honor.

If you encounter a bobcat, do not try to catch them or pet them. Don't try to approach it or try to feed it. Respect it as a wild animal. Bobcats are, indeed, the *ghost of the woods*.

REVIEW

1. Why are bobcats given their common name?

2. What two main characteristics distinguish the bobcat from its cousin, the lynx??

3. Though bobcats eat all kinds of animals, what type of animal do they especially like to eat?

4. Where are bobcats generally found?

5. Explain why it is unusual for a person to see a bobcat?

6. How are bobcats so skillful at catching their prey?

7. What permits a bobcat to be able to walk without making any noise?

8. What size territory does the male bobcat often have?

9. When do the young adolescent bobcats usually leave home to create their own territory?

10. What did you find most fascinating about bobcats?

BOBCAT

bobcat from dailycoloringpages.com

COLORING PAGE

The bobcat cousin, called a lynx.

Name:____________________

Bobcats: Ghostly Elusives

Carefully read the clue and complete the puzzle. Refer to the text if necessary.

Created using the Crossword Maker on TheTeachersCorner.net

nocturnal extirpation crepuscular round tom queen lynx endemic urban

America tail deer solitary hind tuft cat ghost captivity

Across

3. Name given to a male bobcat.
4. Another word for 'native.'
7. Legs that provide bobcats with power and jumping ability.
8. To be active during twilight (dusk and dawn).
13. Pupils in bobcats.
14. Feline; family of bobcats.
15. Longest living bobcat in _______ was 32 years of age.
17. '_________ of the woods'

Down

1. Name given to a female bobcat.
2. Found throughout most of Mexico and North ___________.
3. From which the bobcat gets its name.
5. Favorite food of bobcats.
6. To be active at night.
9. To become extinct in a particular area or environment.
10. That which threatens bobcat existence is called _________ sprawl.
11. Cousin to the bobcat.
12. To be or live alone.
16. A bunch or collection of hairs on the ears.

INTERESTING SOURCES TO CONSIDER

10 True Facts about Bobcats for Kids with Audio. Available at: https://youtu.be/F54-oDtEriM

American Expedition: Bobcat Facts. Available at: https://forum.americanexpedition.us/bobcat-facts-information-and-photos

Animal Fact Friday at Wildlife Prairie Park. Available at: https://youtu.be/4HwfOhZeAHc

Bobcat City: Studying Urban Cats – Texas Parks and Wildlife. Available at: https://youtu.be/0mbGhS9ZNhQ

Bobcat Rescue: Bobcat Facts. Available at: https://bigcatrescue.org/bobcat-facts/

Bring on the Bobcats. National Geographic. Available at: https://youtu.be/IOfbRzg4bQ4

Cool Kid Facts: Bobcat Facts. Available at: https://www.coolkidfacts.com/bobcat-facts/

National Geographic: Bobcat. Available at: https://www.nationalgeographic.com/animals/mammals/b/bobcat/

The Mystery and Magic of Bobcats. Available at: https://youtu.be/eIAEy5aOb9g

ABOUT THE AUTHOR

Richard NeSmith is a native of Florida, USA. He grew up wading through the swamps of central Florida with his two younger brothers during the pre-Disney era and unknowingly falling in love with biology, wildlife, and nature. He has lived in seven American states, twice in Australia and once in Mexico City. He holds eight university degrees and has taught for 14 years in secondary schools, here and abroad, and another 13 years as professor in several American universities. His service includes professor of science education, Dean of Education, Campus Dean, as well as an online instructor. His passion for learning (and *how we learn*) did not develop until *after* graduating from high school. His only explanation for this is that *having a goal made all the difference in the world*. He enjoys reading, hiking, nature photography, golf, and tennis.

New releases of educational and wildlife/naturalist books by Dr. Richard NeSmith.

Recommended book for teachers, parents,

and school administrators!

Applied Principles of Education & Learning

APE-Learning   http://richardnesmith.obior.cc/

Available on Amazon.com at

https://amzn.to/325p92Y

https://bit.ly/2NlleuH

http://amazon.com/author/richardnesmith

[i] Special thanks to the following who kindly provided permission to use their photographs on pixaby.com (David Mark, Amber Steven, Joel Santana Joelfotos, and Jaclyn Wildcat). In addition, special thanks **to Greg Jowers, Ken Buckley, Tom Dotson, David Peters** and **Jim McCarty**, and **Big Cat Rescue.org**. And, as always, special thanks to **Dr. Laurie Aleixo**, for her relief work, her photographs, and her support and encouragement. Finally, *a special thank you to Esther Milez for her wonderful photograph used to create the book cover. Thank you all.*